EPHESUS

REHBER BASIM YAYIN DAĞITIM
REKLAMCILIK VE TİCARET A.Ş.

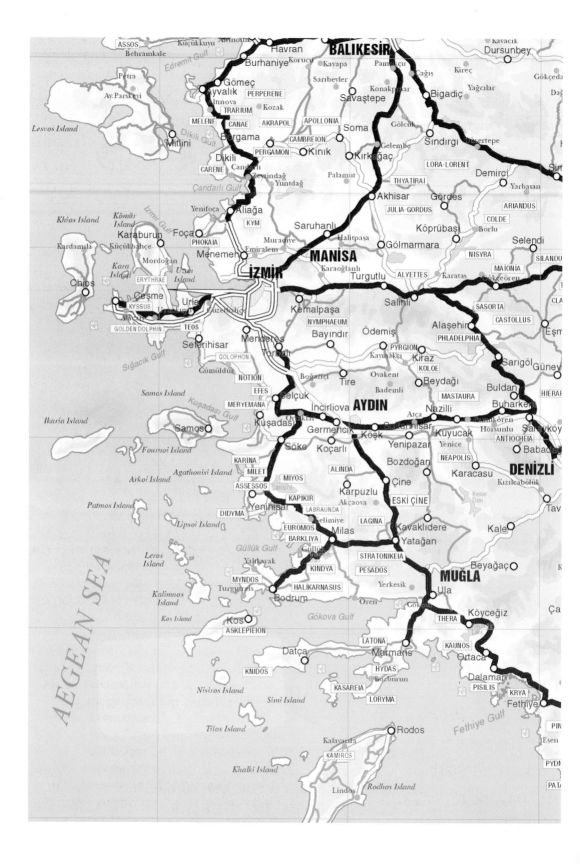

General view of Kuşadası

> "The Ionians who assembled at the panionion founded their cities under the most beautiful sky and in the finest climate in the known world.„

Herodotus of Halicarnassus

> "Ionia; the cradle of empirical science„

Cevat Şakir Kabaağaçlı

"The Fisherman of Halicarnassus".
20th century

I O N I A

According to the "Parian Marble", an inscription on the island of Paros giving the dates of events from the earliest mythological times up to 264 B.C., the Ionian migration took place in 1077 B.C., 301 years before the first Olympic games, while consideration of historical events and written documents allow this migration of the Ionians to Anatolia to be dated to 1200-1050 B.C. Prior to the Aegean migrations, Western Anatolia had been inhabited by indigenous peoples known as the Lelegians, Pelasgians and Carians. A number of settlements had been founded on the coast from Troy to Halicarnassus. It would appear that the Troiad was peopled by the Aeolians and the Halicarnassus region by the Dorians, with the Ionians in the central regions. According to ancient Greek sources, the Ionians were

Peninsula of Çeşme, Sığacık Harbour.

led by Androclus, the son of Codrus, king of Athens, who is also regarded as the founder of the city of Ephesus. According to traditional sources, the Athenians, who formed the main body of the migrants, met with fierce resistance from the local inhabitants and were able to settle in Anatolia only after a series of very bloody wars.

The Ionian cities comprised Priene, Miletus, Teos, Chios, Clazomenae, Myus, Samos, Phocaea, Lebedus, Ephesus, Colophon and Erythrae. According to Herodotus, they all spoke the same language but employed four different dialects. The most southerly of the Ionian towns was Miletus, next came Myus and Priene, all three in Caria and all three speaking the same dialect. Ephesus, Colophon, Lebedus, Teos, Clazomenae and Phocaea were in Lydia and shared a common dialect quite different from that spoken at the above-mentioned places. Chios and Erythrae spoke the same language, and Samos a peculiar one of its own." The Ionian cities were ruled first of all by kings and later by oligarchies, but, in the course of time, some of the cities succeeded in winning popular political rights. During this period the goddess Artemis become the must important goddess of western Anatolia, wheres Athena played a parallel role in contemporary Greece. At that time, the economy was based on agriculture and animal-raising. In his verses Homer mentions vineyards, orchards, vegetable gardens and olive groves, and it would appear that olive oil was used both for cooking and illumination. We learn that Colophon was famed for horse breeding. The first city states (poloi) known to history were founded in Ionia, and by the time Homer wrote his epics they had come to dominate the whole of Ionia. The lacelike coastline of Western Anatolia with its series of bays and coves offered ideal harbours for maritime traffic.

The Phocaeans were pre-eminent in maritime trade, their fifty-oar vessels keeping them in commercial contact with Egypt, while at the same time they founded colonies on the Black Sea and the Sea of Marmara. They later spread as far as the coasts of Italy, Spain and southern France, carrying Ionian culture with them wherever they went. Ports with sheltered harbours soon developed into important centres of trade and commerce. At the beginning of the 8th century B.C. commercial contacts with the Phoenicians led to familiarity with the Phoenician script. The Ionian alphabet was the most important of the eastern branches of the old Greek alphabet and the form employed in the city of Miletus was adopted as the official alphabet in Athens in 403 B.C. In the middle of the 4th century B.C. this became the twenty-four letter Greek alphabet of the classical period. At the same time, remarkable progress was made in oral literature. These epics, handed on by word of mouth from one generation to the next, finally gave rise, in the middle of the 8th century, to works such as the Iliad and the Odyssey, in which Homer, a native of Smyrna, employed a mixture of the Ionian and Aeolian dialects. Ionia also developed as one of the most influential centres of oracular prophecy in the Greek world with the fame of the temples of Claros and Didyma spreading throughout the whole of the Mediterranean region. The greatest contribution made by the Lydians, who dominated the region in the 7th and 6th centuries, was the introduc-tion of coinage as a means of exchange. Coinage of electrum

The ancient city of Priene. Temple of Athena.

(an alloy of 60% gold and 40% silver) made its way through the Ionian and Aegean regions, reaching as far as Greece itself.

It was in Ionia that rule by tyrants first emerged. The word "tyrant" is derived from the Lydian language, where it means "lord". From this time on, Ionia was the most important centre of the various branches of philosophy, literature and art, while at the same time cultural activities ceased to be the monopoly of the aristocracy and began to spread   amongst the common people.

The music of Lydia and Phrygia played an important role in the development of the lyrical poetry of the 7th century B.C., and lyric poems began to be sung throughout the Greek world to the accompaniment of the lyre and the flute. In the 6th century, philosophy began to be cultivated in intellectual circles and scientific laws began to be formulated for the explanation of

natural phenomena, thus laying the foundation of modern science.

The Ionic order appeared in the field of architecture and the Ionic style soon spread far beyond the borders of Ionia to the shores of Greece and the southern Mediterranean and even Persia, the influence of Ionian architecture being clearly visible in the Persian palaces. Temples in the Ionic style are characterised by tall, slender columns, with fluted shafts.

The most magnificent example of this style of architecture was to be found in the Temple of Artemis at Ephesus. The defeat of the Lydian monarchy by the Persians led to a radical shift in the balance of political power in Western Anatolia and in 545 B.C. all the coastal cities came under Persian hegemony.

The coastal city of Çeşme, one of the most important tourist centres in the Aegean region.

IONIAN THINKERS

In the 6th century B.C. Ionia produced a number of thinkers who devoted themselves to the study of the universe and the discovery of the laws of nature. In this way they broke the chains of religion and bigotry which had existed up to that time and showed that natural phenomena were governed, not by mysterious forces but by natural laws. Thus it was in Ionia that the first signs appeared of an age of enlightenment in Anatolia. These thinkers have come to be known as the "Ionian natural philosophers".

HERACLEITUS (540-480 B.C.)

Heracleitus was born and brought up in Ephesus. He concentrated on the problem of existence. He believed that fire was the essence of the universe, and also believed in the transitory nature of all things, the apparent permanence and stability of things within this actual transitoriness being mere illusion. The appearance of permanency arises from the fact that change is governed not by chance but by certain laws and takes place in accordance with a certain order. Heracleitus named this order "LOGOS". The universe is governed by law and it is the task of reason to discover this law.

ANAXAGORAS

A native of Clazomenae (Güladası), Anaxagoras was one of the most important of the 5th century thinkers. In 462 he went to Athens, where he spent the next thirty years of his life. He won fame as a mathematician, while at the same time making some very important discoveries in astronomy. He explained the problem of the light from the moon and of the eclipse of the sun and moon.

According to Anaxagoras there were many elements distinguished by different qualities produced not by the entry into the compound of new elements but by the separation of elements in the compounds.

He introduced the idea of the atom and its possible separation. He was sentenced to death in Athens for denying the divinity of the sun and moon and declaring that they consisted of masses of material.

XENOPHANES (569-477 B.C.)

A contemporary of Heracleitus, Xenophanes was a native of the city of Colophon. He might be regarded as a religious teacher rather than a philosopher.

He opposed the anthromorphic approach to the gods. He believed in a single god of a wholly intellectual nature, a philosophical approach that constituted the first step on the road towards monotheism.

DEMOCRITUS (460-390 B.C.)

Democritus was a native of Teos. Only a few fragments of his works have survived. He declared that a single scientific discovery was worth more than being King of Persia. According to Democritus, nothing disappears or changes its form, it always remains the same. But besides being, there is also non-being, i.e. empty space. According to Democritus, matter is composed of indivisible, invisible particles distinguished in form, position in space, size and weight. These particles Democritus called "atoms".

Democritus thus laid the foundations of a mechanist approach to natural philosophy, but in ancient times his views were to remain undeveloped. His approach to natural philosophy was taken up again only at the beginning of the modern age. He was the first to discover the law of cause and effect.

THALES (625-545 B.C.)

Thales is recognised as the founder of Western philosophy. He believed that water formed the essence of matter, and is renowned for having forecast the eclipse of the sun that took place on the 28 May 585 B.C. He died at the age of seventy-eight during the 58th Olympic Games. None of his writings have survived. He advised sailors to take their bearings from the LITTLE DIPPER rather than the BIG DIPPER formed by the northern stars. He is said to have used geometry to calculate the height of the Egyptian pyramids and the distance of a ship from the shore. He is universally agreed to have foreseen the eclipse of the sun which brought the battle between the Lydian King Alyattes and Cyaxares, King of the Medes, to an end. He was the discoverer of a number of geometrical theorems. 1. The diameter divides the circumference into two equal sections, 2. The two angles at the base of an isosceles triangle are equal, 3. The opposite angles at the point of intersection of two straight lines are equal. 4. Two straight lines from a point on the circumference of a circle to the ends of the diameter form a right angle. Thales' material approach to the universe constituted a break with traditional mythological explanations. Both sides in the battle mentioned above broke off hostilities in the belief that this was a sign from the gods. Thales had calculated the time of the eclipse beforehand and informed the Lydians accordingly.

Sayings:

- Do not enrich yourself by shameful means.
- Expect as much help in your old age as you yourself have given to your parents in your youth.

General view of the city of Izmir.

I Z M I R

Izmir is located in the Aegean province, which, of all the seven geographical regions of Turkey, enjoys the finest climate. In population it is the third city in Turkey.

It is located in an area whose magnificent history has made it a tourist centre. It lies at the centre of the most important land, air and sea communication network in the ancient Aegean region.

THE LEGENDARY ORIGIN
OF ITS NAME:

The wife of Cinyras, King of Cyprus, foolishly claimed that her daughter, Smyrna, was more beautiful than Aphrodite herself. This so enraged the goddess that she made Smyrna fall in love with her own father and one night, Smyrna's nurse having made the

The Clock-Tower. The emblem of Izmir.

king drunk, she climbed into his bed. When he finally awoke from his drunken slumber, the king drew his sword and drove his daughter from the palace, pursuing her into the countryside.

Just as he was about to overtake her and kill her with his sword, Aphrodite took pity on the girl and turned her into a myrrh tree.

As it descended, the king's sword split the myrrh-tree and ADONIS tumbled out. And thus Adonis was born.

According to famous ancient travellers such as Aristides, Strabo, Pliny and Pausanias, Izmir was founded around 1450 B.C. by TANTALUS, King of Manisa (Spilos) to the north-east of the present-day city.

There is also a legend to the effect that it was founded by the Amazons. The one certain thing is that Izmir is not a Greek word and would appear to be derived from an autochthonous language.

HISTORY:

The excavations carried out in 1948 by the British Archaeological Institute of Athens and, after 1960, by the Turkish Historical Association under Prof. Ekrem Akurgal have shown that the first settlement, known as Bayraklı, can be dated as far back as the Bronze Age (3500-1000 B.C.)

The remains of the earliest layer are contemporary with the Troy II civilization. This settlement was known as Smurna, written as Smyrna in ancient Greek.

In the 11th century B.C. the coastal city of Smyrna was inhabited by Ionians and Aeolians.

The mudbrick defence walls, which have been dated to the 8th century B.C., indicate that Izmir was already a city state at that time. The Temple of Athena, thought to have been built between the years 725-700 B.C., is the most ancient example of Greek architecture in the East.

Also to be found here is the oldest specimen of a Greek house, with courtyard in front, and five rooms on two storeys. Smyrna also boasts the oldest example of a cobbled street in Greek civilisation.

The tomb of TANTALUS (Tholos) on Mt Yamanlar is one of the oldest examples of a circular tomb.

In the 8th and 7th centuries B.C. the region came under the rule of the Phrygians and Lydians. The city, which had been destroyed during that period, was captured by the Persians in the 6th century and once again destroyed. In 333 B.C. it fell into the hands of Alexander the Great.

The city could no longer be contained within its old defence walls and was re-founded on Mt Pagos, now known as Kadifekale. By the 1st century B.C. only a small part of the city remained on Mt Pagos, the greater part lying in the vicinity of the harbour.

In 288 B.C. the city became subject to the Kingdom of Pergamon and, on the death of King Attalos III in 133 B.C. it became part of the Roman Empire in accordance with the terms of Attalos' will.

In the 7th century A.D. it was exposed to raids by the Arabs.

By the 9th century the city had become a Byzantine naval base with a dockyard. Under the Nicaean Empire (1204-1260) it was an important international port.

The first Turkish conquest of the city took place towards the end of the 11th century during the reign of Kutalmışoğlu Süleyman Shah, and in 1426 it was incorporated into Ottoman territory.

The fort on the shore was rebuilt by Mehmed the Conqueror after an attack by the Venetians in 1472 .

The first textile factory was opened in the 18th century and the first paper factory in the 19th.

On 15 May 1919 the occupation of the city by the Greeks sparked off the Turkish national struggle for Independence.

On its liberation in 1922 three-quarters of the city was destroyed by fire. The industrialisation and urbanisation that characterised the years following the proclamation of the Republic destroyed the lovely landscape that the city had formerly possessed. Today, the old city slumbers in oblivion in a growing and rapidly changing Izmir, but those really interested can still find old houses with bay windows hidden away in narrow streets, old Ottoman hans and magnificent Levantine mansions, as well as old mosques, synagogues and churches.

At the beginning of the 20th century Izmir was a centre of commerce and entertainment rivalling Istanbul and Salonica in the hierarchy of Ottoman cities and famous for its raisins and seedless grapes, its almonds, its horse-drawn phaetons, its spring festival, its "gold drop" Eau de Cologne and *nargiles* or water-pipes. The population of 200,000 at the turn of the century has now grown to 3 million. All types of cottons and textiles, together with agricultural produce such as tobacco, grapes, figs, olives and olive oil are exported from Izmir to all four corners of the world. Today the city retains its importance as the largest export harbour in Turkey.

PLACES OF INTEREST :
ST POLYCARP CHURCH

St Polycarp, one of the disciples of the Evangelist St John, arrived in Izmir in 80 A.D. He was crucified and burned by the Romans for his dissemination of Christianity and a white dove is said to have flown up into the sky from the spot where he died.

Now there is a church, which is used by the catholic minority both as a place of worship and a place of pilgrimage. The present building dates from around 1690. At the beginning of the century the murals were restored by the French architect Raymond Pee.

11

* The city's oldest house was built in 1715. This is an excellent example of a house with overhangs. It is located in the Namazgâh district.

ATATÜRK MUSEUM

The old NAIM PALAS HOTEL, a typical Izmir *köşk* converted into a hotel in 1862, became the army headquarters in the last years of the Independence Struggle. Presented by the Municipality of Izmir to Atatürk In 1927, it was converted after his death into a museum and opened to the public in 1940. It contains Atatürk's personal belongings, photographs, oil paintings, marble and bronze busts, as well as a caique which he had used.

ARCHAEOLOGICAL MUSEUM

The museum, which was transferred to its present building in 1984, contains finds yielded by excavations in various parts of the region, such as Bayraklı, Ephesus, Pergamum, Miletus, Aphrodisias, Sardis and Iasos, all arranged in chronological order and ranging in date from 1000 B.C. to Ottoman times.

Outstanding exhibits include the statues of Demeter and Zeus from the Agora in Izmir, geometric pottery, Yortan type vessels, Sidamara sarcophagi and column capitals. There are over ten thousand exhibits in all.

KIZILÇULLU AQUEDUCT

The aqueduct was constructed to bring water from the Ak and Karapınar springs on Mt Nif to the city. It is a Late Roman structure dating from the 2nd century A.D. which underwent repairs during the Ottoman period.

AGORA

This underwent repairs in the 2nd century

Izmir. The corniche at Alsancak.

Remains of the Izmir Agora sculpture of Demeter and Poseidon.

Two ancient heads. Eros and a priest.

A.D. It was located underneath a cemetery in the district known as Namazgâh or Tilkilik on the skirts of Kadifekale. Only the northern and western sections have been excavated. In the northern section there is a basilica 160 m in length with three aisles divided by two rows of columns supporting a sloping roof. The pink marble was brought from the Karaburun Mts. built on the slope of a hill. The building has deep foundations with arches and vaults raising the lower floor to ground level.

CLOCK TOWER

The clock tower was erected by the Grand Vizier Küçük Sait Pasha in 1901 to celebrate the 25th anniversary of Abdülhamid II's accession to the throne. The clock itself was presented by the German Emperor Wilhelm II. The tower is 25 m in height.

ATATÜRK MONUMENT

Located in Republic Square, the monument was erected in 1932 by the Italian sculptor Pietro Canonica. On the pedestal is the relief inscription, *"Ordular. İlk hedefimiz Akdeniz!"* (Troops. Our first target is the Mediterranean!). There are also reliefs depicting scenes from the War of Independence.

IZMIR FAIR

The idea of an international fair, first mooted at the Economic Congress of 1923, was first realised in 1936 with the support of Atatürk. An annual event, it is now located in the natural setting of the Culture Park.

CABLE CAR

This is located in 302nd St. in the district in which the famous singer DARIO MORENO once lived. It offers visitors an unrivalled view of Izmir.

General view of the Izmir Agora.

Statue of Atatürk in Cumhuriyet square and Konak mosque in Konak square.

The Izmir Büyük Efes Hotel.

H O M E R

The life and works of Homer, the earliest epic poet whose works have survived, still give rise to a great deal of discussion and controversy. According to Herodotus of Halicarnassus, he lived around 850 B.C., and it is generally agreed that he was born in Izmir, lived on the island of Chios and died in Ios. Some believe that in the Aeolian dialect the word "homer" means "blind". Obvious differences in style and technique between the two epics, the Iliad and the Odyssey, have led some scholars to believe that they are the works of different poets. Homer's epics have been known since the 7th century and in the 6th century parts are known to have been read in the Panathena Festival in Athens. Throughout the whole of the Hellenistic and Roman periods Homer's epics were regarded as sacred texts. According to Aristotle and Strabo, copies of the two works had been prepared by Anaxorchos and Callisthenes. Alexander the Great found them in the war booty seized from Darius and preserved them in a coffer of peerless value. The Iliad, which consists of some 16,000 verses, covers the last forty days of the war between the Trojans and the Achaeans. The Odyssey, a poem of 12,000 verses, covers the ten years following the end of the war and relates the adventures of Odyssey and his companions during their return from Troy. The Odyssey is said to have been written fifty years later than the Iliad. The influence of Homer, which greatly increased in the West at the time of the Renaissance, continues unabated at the present day.

MOSQUES

Hisar Mosque: This, the largest mosque in izmir, is said to have been built in 1598.

Başdurak Mosque: According to the 17th century traveller Evliya Çelebi it was built in 1652.

Kestane Pazarı Mosque: Built in 1668.

Çorak Kapı Mosque in the Basmane district, said to have been built in 1747.

KONAK (YALI) MOSQUE: Located in front of the Government House it was built in 1754.

KURŞUNLU MOSQUE: The oldest mosque in the city, it is thought to have been built in the 16th century by Sultan Selim I.

SHADIRVAN MOSQUE: Built in the 16th century.

KIZLARAĞASI MOSQUE: Thought to have been built in 1745. Built on the plan of a market han.

Foça, one of the most important of the ancient sites of Ionia.

Karaburun, Çeşme.

Kuşadası, the busiest port in present-day Ionia.

K U Ş A D A S I

Kuşadası is the most important centre of tourism in the province of Ionia on the coast of the Aegean, and the most lively holiday resort after Antalya on the Mediterranean shores of Turkey.

All this is due to its location as the first stop on the touristic voyages down the western coast and its proximity to the Greek island of Samos, from which thousands of trippers arrive every day, more particularly in order to visit the ruins of Ephesus.

The history of Kuşadası can be traced back to the Trojan War at the end of the 2nd millennium B.C. King Agamemnon is thought to have founded the ancient Pygeyla as a military base, but the site as a centre of habitation dates from the Hellenistic period. In the 3rd century B.C. the city enjoyed a period of great brilliance as a summer resort for the wealthy citizens of Ephesus.

The earliest mention of Marathesion, as Kuşadası was then known, is to be found in the works of the celebrated ancient geographer and traveller Strabo.

In the Middle Ages, Kuşadası, then known as "Scala Nova", was a coastal city of great importance frequented more particularly by the Venetian and Genoese merchants. After its capture by the Ottomans it retained it importance as a naval base and in the 16th century a castle and arsenal were constructed on the island which gave the city its name and which is now connected to the mainland by a causeway. In the 17th century the rapidly developing commercial activity led to the erection of the fairly large caravanserai known as the Öküz Mehmet Pasha Kervansaray, which now stands in the centre of Kuşadası, while in the first half of the 19th century the castle was renovated,

18

General views of Kuşadası.

enlarged and strengthened.

Following the tourism explosion which took place comparatively recently in Turkey, Kuşadası, which, until the 1970s, remained a quiet, peaceful, very charming little country town, has displayed a quite remarkable development as a touristic centre, with glorious beaches stretching for 50 km along the coast line.

As an economic and commercial centre with hundreds of hotels, motels, holiday villages, pensions, etc., Kuşadası is now in danger of being buried under a flood of concrete.

Ephesus, the Agora.

The ancient city of Ephesus. The Marble Way, the Agora and the Library of Celsus.

E P H E S U S

· According to the old legends, Ephesus was founded by the female warriors known as the Amazons. The name of the city is thought to have been derived from "APASAS", the name of a city in the "KINGDOM OF ARZAWA" meaning the "city of the Mother Goddess". Ephesus was inhabited from the end of the Bronze Age onwards, but changed its location several times in the course of its long history in accordance with habits and requirements. Carians and Lelegians are to be have been among the city's first inhabitants. Ionian migrations are said to have begun in around 1200 B.C. According to legend, the city was founded for the second time by Androclus, the son of Codrus, king of Athens, on the shore at the point where the CAYSTER (Küçük Menderes) empties into the sea, a location to which they had been guided by a fish and a wild boar on the advice of the soothsayers. The Ionian cities that grew up in the wake of the Ionian migrations joined in a confederacy under the leadership of Ephesus. The region was devastated during the Cimmerian invasion at the beginning of the 7th century B.C. Under the rule of the Lydian kings, Ephesus became one of the wealthiest cities in the Mediterranean world. The defeat of the Lydian King Croesus by Cyrus, the King of Persia, prepared the way for the extension of Persian hegemony over the whole of the Aegean coastal region. At the beginning of the 5th century, when the Ionian cities rebelled against Persia, Ephesus quickly dissociated itself from the others, thus escaping destruction.

Ephesus remained under Persian rule until the arrival of Alexander the Great in 334 B.C., when it entered upon a fifty year period of peace and tranquillity. Lysimachus, who had been one of the twelve generals of Alexander the Great and became ruler of the region on Alexander's death, decided to embark upon the development of the city, which he called Arsineia after his wife Arsinoë. He constructed a new harbour and built defence walls on the slopes of the Panayır and Bülbül Mts., moving the whole city 2.5 km to the south-west. Realising, however, that the Ephesians were unwilling to leave their old city, he had the whole sewage system blocked up during a great storm, making the houses uninhabitable and forcing the inhabitants to move. In 281 B.C. the city was re-founded under the old name of Ephesus and became one of the most important of the commercial ports in the Mediterranean.

In 129 B.C. the Romans took advantage of the terms of the will left by Attalos, King of Pergamon, by which they were bequathed his kingdom, to incorporate the whole region into the Roman Empire as the province of Asia. Ancient sources show that

The Street of Curetes and Library of Celsus.

at this time the city had a population of 200,000. In the 1st century B.C. the heavy taxes imposed by the Roman government led the population to embrace Mithridates as their saviour and to support him in his mutiny against Roman authority and in 88 B.C. a massacre was carried out of all the Latin speaking inhabitants of the city, which was then stormed and sacked by a Roman army under Sulla, It was from the reign of Augustus onwards that the buildings we admire today were constructed. According to documentary sources, the city suffered severe damage in an earthquake in 17 A.D. After that, however, Ephesus became a very important centre of trade and commerce. The historian Aristio describes Ephesus as being recognised by all the inhabitants of the region as the most important trading centre in Asia. It was also the leading political and intellectual centre, with the second school of philosophy in the Aegean. From the 1st century onwards, Ephesus was visited by Christian disciples attempting to spread the Christian belief in a single God and thus forced to seek refuge from Roman persecution. Besides enjoying a privileged position between East and West coupled with an exceptionally fine climate, the city owed its importance to its being the centre of the cult of Artemis.

For the Christians, the city, with its highly advanced way of life, its high standard of living, the variety of its demographic composition and its firmly rooted polytheistic culture, must have presented itself as an ideal pilot region… From written sources we learn that St Paul remained in the city for three years from 65 to 68, and that it was here that he preached his famous sermons calling upon the hearers to embrace the faith in one God. He taught that God had no need of a house made with human hands and that he was present in all places at all times. This was all greatly resented by the craftsmen who had amassed great wealth from their

The Temple of Hadrian, The Street of Curetes and Library of Celsus.

production of statues of Artemis in gold, silver or other materials. A silversmith by the name of Demetrius stirred up the people and led a crowd of thousands of Ephesians to the theatre, where they booed and stoned Paul and his two colleagues, chanting "Great is Artemis of the Ephesians! Great is Artemis of the Ephesians!" So turbulent was the crowd that Paul and his companions escaped only with great difficulty. From his Epistles to the communities it would appear that Paul spent some time as a prisoner in Ephesus.

Legend has it that St John the Evangelist came to Ephesus with the Virgin Mary in his care. Some also say that it was here that he wrote his Gospel and was finally buried. In 269 Ephesus and the surrounding country was devastated by the Goths. At that time there was still a temple in which the cult of Artemis was practised. In 381, by order of the Emperor Theodosius, the temple was

closed down, and in the following centuries it lay completely abandoned, serving as a quarry for building materials.

The situation of the city, which had given it its privileged geographical position, was also the cause of its decline and fall. The prosperity of the city had been based on its possession of a sheltered natural harbour, but by the Roman period ships reached the harbour to the west of Mt Pion 1.5 km from the Temple of Artemis through a very narrow and difficult channel. The cause of this was the Meander (Cayster) River, which emptied into the Aegean a little to the west of the city of Ephesus, where it created a delta formed by the alluvium carried down by the river over thousands of years. By the late Byzantine era the channel had been so silted up as to be no longer usable. The sea gradually receded farther and farther, while the marshy lands around the harbour gave

The ancient city of Ephesus. The Great Theatre from the Harbour Road.

Fountain of Trajan.

rise to a number of diseases, such as malaria. The new outlook that had arisen with the spread of Christianity led to the gradual abandonment of all buildings bearing witness to the existence of polytheistic cults and the construction in their place of Christian churches. In the year 431 the third Ecumenical council took place in Ephesus.

Emperor Theodosius convoked another council in Ephesus in 449, which came to be known as the "robber council". From the 6th century onwards the Church of St John was an important place of pilgrimage, and Justinian took measures to protect it by having the whole hill on which it stood surrounded by defence walls. Shortly afterwards, the Church of the Virgin and other places of worship were destroyed and pillaged in Arab raids. In the 7th century the city was transferred to the site now occupied by the town of Selçuk and during the

Byzantine era Ephesus grew up around the summit of Mt Ayasuluğ. The city enjoyed its last years of prosperity under the Seljuk Emirate of the Aydınoğulları. During the Middle Ages the city ceased to function as a port.

By the 20th century the silt carried down by the Meander had extended the plain for a distance of 5 km.

EXCAVATIONS AT EPHESUS

The first excavations were carried out in 1859-74 on the odeon and the theatre by J.T.Wood under the auspices of the British Museum. Excavations were carried out on the Temple of Artemis in May 1869. Regular excavations began in 1895 under the direction of Otto Bendore, a member of the Viennese Academy. The excavations directed by R.Heberg on behalf of the Austrian Archaeological Institute uncovered the

View of one of the camel-wrestling held annually in the Stadium.

Agora, the Theatre, the Arcadiane and the Library of Celsus. Operations were suspended during the First World War, but work was resumed in 1926. Excavations were conducted by a large team under the direction of Hermann Vetters on behalf of the Austrian Archaeological Institute.

Owing to the dense and continuous nature of the Roman settlement it was only in 1960 that the Hellenistic layers were reached.

RUINS

Present-day visitors wishing to visit the Hellenistic and Roman remains at Ephesus have a choice between two entrances. If they arrive from the direction of Kuşadası they will enter Ephesus from the harbour gate. In that case the first building the visitor encounters will be:

THE GYMNASIUM OF VEDIUS

This gymnasium was built in 150 A.D. by Vedius Antonius, a wealthy citizen of Ephesus. According to an inscription discovered during excavations on the eastern facade of the building the gymnasium was dedicated to Artemis and the consul Antonius Pius. The most important of the chambers opening off the palaestra contained a cult statue of the emperor. A large number of statues were found, among them two sculptures of the river god now exhibited in the Izmir Archaeological Museum. The latrine is in a very good state of preservation.

STADIUM

The stadium, which is located immediately to the south of the gymnasium, was built by the Emperor Nero (54-68 A.D.). The whole measures 228 x 38 m., with the tiers of seats resting against the slope of Mt Panayır and the northern section of the cavea supported by vaults. The finds include a number of column capitals and roughly carved marble slabs. The building was later used as a quarry for building materials for use in the construction of the Byzantine castle, with the result that very little now remains.

The stadium was used for chariot races, athletic displays and gladiatorial combats and marble reliefs depicting gladiators are displayed along the Marble Way. In the hilly terrain opposite the stadium a number of buildings of uncertain date have been unearthed. These include a fish market, a Byzantine fountain and a funeral chamber thought to be that of Androcles, the legendary founder of the city. The Marble Way (Via tecta) connecting the Artemision to the centre of the city, passed by here. The stadium is now used for the camel wrestling competitions which have gradually become a traditional feature. Every year, in spring, visitors come from all over the country for the festivities taking place during the annual fair.

ROMAN BOURSE or DOUBLE CHURCH OF THE VIRGIN MARY:

This Roman building is dated to the 2nd century A.D. It is a three-aisled church measuring 265 x 90 m. Until its conversion into a church in the 4th century A.D. it performed a secular function. Its proximity to the harbour allowed important commercial goods to be marketed here without the necessity of transporting them into the city itself. The Byzantine church was added to the western side.

Austrian archaeologists are engaged here in endeavours to locate the site of the

Camel-wrestling contest in the Stadium with peasants in local costumes.

The ancient city of Ephesus. The Double Church of the Virgin Mary.

bishop's palace. The church itself housed the third Ecumenical counsil at which the divine character of Christ and the Virgin Mary was discussed. Nestorius (380-451), the founder of the school of Antioch and the Patriarchate of Istanbul, put forward the view opposing the divine nature of Christ and regarding Mary not as the mother of God but as the mother of a human being. The Alexandrian school, on the other hand, put foward the more mystical, more traditional view that Mary was the mother of God and in the end Nestorius was exiled. Ephesus thus became one of the most important centres of the Christian world and the reverence for the Virgin Mary at Ephesus was greatly increased.

The so called Robber Council of 449 accepted the thesis of the purely divine nature of Christ in which his human character was completely ignored. This doctrine was later known in the East as Monophysitism.

THE ARCADIANE

This street, 600 m long and 11 m wide, was given this name after its restoration by the Emperor Arcadius (395-408). The main street of the city connecting the theatre and the surrounding area to the port, it was flanked by stoas with mosaic floors. These colonnades, which included a row of shops, served to protect the inhabitants of the   city from wind and rain in the winter and from the sun in the summer. Inscriptions on four imposing Corinthian columns erected by the Emperor Justinian (525-566) indicate the existence of sculptures of the four Evangelists. An inscription in the theatre informs us that the street was illuminated by two rows of torches.

The Great Theatre.

Scene from the Ephesus Festival in the Great Theatre.

The brothel sign carved in the marble on the Marble Way.

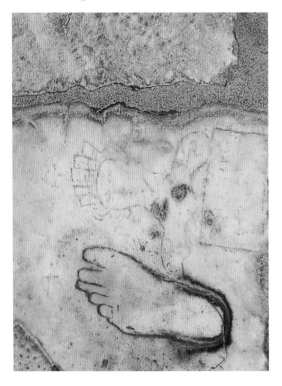

THE THEATRE:

The theatre is built against the slope of Mt Panayir. It has now lost most of its imposing decoration. It was one of the largest theatres in the Aegean world, measuring 60 m from the floor of the stage to the top of the galleries. The cavea consists of three sections. The auditorium held 24,000 spectators with another thousand in the vaulted galleries, making up a total capacity of over 25,000. Massive alterations to the original auditorium would appear to have been undertaken during the reign of Claudius and completed under the Emperor Trajan. The tiers of seats were later used as spolia in the construction of other buildings. The first and second storeys of the stage building were constructed during the reign of Nero (54-68), while the third storey was constructed during the reign of Septimus Severus (193-211). The stage facade was

The Marble Way.

The Mazeus-Mithridates Gate.

adorned with niches, columns, reliefs and statues. The stage was at a height of 2.70 m above the orchestra and was reached by ramps on the left and right.

THE MARBLE WAY

he Marble Way connects the theatre to the Library of Celsus. It assumed its present-day appearance during the 5th century A.D. Drains were installed throughout the whole length of the street in the form of lower galleries. A few reliefs on the ground on the right hand side indicate the city brothel. The reliefs include a left foot, the portrait of a woman and a heart decorated with perforations. They are surrounded by an iron railing.

THE GATE OF MAZAEUS AND MITHRIDATES

This gate, built almost entirely of marble, was dedicated in 3 B.C. to Augustus and his son-in-law Agrippa by two rich freedmen of the city Mazeus and Mithridates. These two imposing gates leading into the agora constitute the finest example of restoration work carried out in recent years.

AGORA

Originally built in the 1st century B.C. it was in the form of an open-air market-place measuring 110 x 110 m. Repaired by the Emperor Caracalla at the beginning of the 3rd century, it was reduced to more or less the state we see it in today by a great earthquake in the 4th century. The largest centre of commerce in the city, foodstuffs and all sorts of manufactured goods were bought and sold here. The shops were arranged along the colonnades and opened into vaulted storerooms at the back. A water clock and sundial were placed in the middle of the agora.

LIBRARY OF CELSUS

Although the building is of a mainly

Library of Celsus.

Views of the Library of Celsus.

Gate of Lower Agora.

cultural character it is also a funerary monument. After the death of Celsus Polemaenus, a former consul who had been appointed governor of Ephesus, his son erected a magnificent reading room over his tomb. The building, which dates from the 2nd century, was attacked by fire in 260 but the facade suffered no damage. It is 21 m wide and 16 m high. Equestrian statues stood on pedestals on each side of the main staircases and there are also indications that statues were placed in the niches on the upper floor. The main room measures 16 x 10 m. The burial chamber under the ground floor contains a sarcophagus in an excellent state of preservation. Excavations carried out by Austrian archaeologists at the beginning of the 20th century revealed a 4th century fountain in the front courtyard and very valuable carvings in high relief depicting the wars waged by Marcus Aurelius and Lucius Verus against the Parthians. Advantage was taken of legal loopholes existing at the time of the excavations to transfer these reliefs, together with four female statues from the facade of the library, to the Kunsthistorische Museum in Vienna.

The monumental facade as it stands today is the result of restoration work begun in the 1970s. Lead plates are placed at the top and bottom of the columns and the whole given a play of 50 cm capable of withstanding a 9 degree earthquake on the east-west axis. A perforation of 10 cm has been made in each of the columns and iron inserted. While work was in progress on the front facade an unknown aspect of Roman architecture was discovered in the form of a curve starting from zero at the bottom of the stairs and reaching 4.5 cm at the bases of the columns. This curve reaches 10 cm in converse fashion, a feature which until now was

Relief of Nike, the Goddess of Victory.

thought to have existed only in Greek architecture. This expedient is known to have been employed in order to increase the monumental effect over an area 21 m in width. Restoration of the building was completed and the whole opened to the public in 1978.

TEMPLE OF SERAPIS

This temple dates from the 2nd century and was dedicated to Serapis, one of the Egyptian gods. It is of considerable importance as evidence of the atmosphere of tolerance that existed in Ephesus, the cosmopolitan character of whose population allowed the proliferation of a number of different religious beliefs. It is built in the Corinthian order, with marble of very high quality, and is remarkable for the size of its monolithic columns, some of them rising to a height of 12 m. A door opening on rollers

gives access to a long cult chamber in which a statue of Egyptian granite is thought to have stood. Some of the monolithic blocks weigh over 50 tonnes. It would appear to have been left unfinished. There are no inscriptions.

BROTHEL

The whole of the present-day complex dates from the 4th century. Situated immediately opposite the Library of Celsus, It consists of rooms and salons grouped around a courtyard measuring 20.5 x 20.5 m. A narrow section gives access to the rooms and salons. On the left hand side of the entrance there was a section in which visitors wiped the mud and dust from their clothes. The houses are adorned with rich and interesting mosaics. The beautiful women are known to have been intellectual and well-educated and, besides enjoying

The Terrace Houses, general view and fresco of a female figure in the theatre room in the peristyle house.

Mosaics in the peristyle house.

Fountain of Polio.

priviliges unknown to the ordinary Roman woman, such as being able to own their own houses and take part in demonstrations and elections, they also had the right to choose their own customers.

LATRINE

This is in a very good state of preservation. It originally consisted of a semi-covered rectangular area surrounded by columns with marble and bronze statues in the centre and a pool affording ventilation. The room is surrounded by a row of marble seats with a marble conduit below it allowing a flow of water. The floor was covered with mosaics and the walls with marble panels. Use of the latrine was restricted to men, who paid a fee on entrance. Public latrines were built in order to obtain the uric acid used in tanning sheep and goatskins in the tanneries opened by the Emperor Vespasian.

TERRACE HOUSES

Some of these houses were first opened to the public in 1985, when restoration work was completed. It has been proved that this sector was used for urban development from the 1st century B.C. onwards. The houses were the property of various owners until the 7th century. The district enjoyed its peak of prosperity between the 2nd and 4th centuries. These were one-storey houses occupied by wealthy citizens or priests of noble lineage and composed of spacious rooms grouped around an open-air courtyard, the largest being used as reception and dining-rooms. In addition to kitchens and cellars a large number of bed-rooms have been unearthed. Water was

Temple of Hadrian.

supplied by fountains surrounded by moisaics. Some of the walls reach a height of 4 m. Stairs leading to the upper storeys have also been unearthed. For flooring, mosaics were preferred to marble pavements but marble was frequently employed in tbe thresholds. Wall decorations consist mainly of painting on plaster. A visit to the terrace houses should be supplemented by a visit to the Archaeological Museum in Selçuk in which a very rich collection of murals, furniture and utensils are exhibited.

SCHOLASTICIA BATHS

These baths date from the 1st century A.D. but were restored and enlarged in the 5th century by a wealthy woman by the name of Scholasticia. The hot room remains in a fairly good state of preservation and the well-preserved statue of the wealthy founder stands on the entrance terrace.

Fountain of Trajan.

Gate of Heracles.

THE STREET OF THE CURETES

This street runs from the Library of Celsus to the Gate of Hercules and thence to the Odeon. On the right, work is in progress on the Gate of Hadrian. In the same road a burial chamber, known as the "Octagon" has been discovered containing the bones of a young woman of about twenty years of age. The building itself has been dated to the 1st century, but marble slabs dating from the 4th century contain inscriptions recording the repairs carried out by the administrators Eutropius and Festus between the years 358 and 368.

THE TEMPLE OF HADRIAN

This Corinthian temple dates from the 2nd century but underwent repairs in the 4th and has recently been re-erected from the surviving architectural fragments. The reliefs in the upper sections are casts, the originals

42

Monument of Memmius.

being now exhibited in the Selçuk Archaeological Museum. The temple is a veritable miracle, a peerless specimen of Roman architecture. A number of interesting figures are depicted in the reliefs, including the Emperor Theodosius I, his wife and eldest son, the Emperor Arcadius accompanied by the goddess Athena (depicted at both ends of the block), Artemis of Ephesus and Androcles stalking a wild boar. In front of the facade stood statues of four important emperors, Diocletian, Constantine, Maximian and Galerius). The pediment with its lacelike carving is adorned with a relief bust of the goddess Tyche. The entrance door is surrounded by an egg design and surmounted by a large Medusa relief.

FOUNTAIN OF TRAJAN

Erected in the 2nd century, it has undergone partial repair. On the front facade there was a life-size statue of Trajan of which only the right foot and a portion of the torso has survived. A sculpture depicting two reclining satyrs and a statue of Aphrodite discovered here are now exhibited in the local museum. It is a two-storey structure 12 m in height surrounding the pool in front on three sides.

GATE OF HERCULES

This is dated to the end of the 4th or the beginning of the 5th century. A block adorned with a relief of Nike, the goddess of victory, now located a little further on, originally stood at this gate, which consists of two blocks of stone with a relief depicting the combat of Hercules and the Nemaean lion. On the terrace immediately to the left of the gate there is a four-columned Hellenistic fountain.

Temple of Domitian.

MONUMENT OF MEMMIUS

This monument was erected by the dictator Sulla in 86 B.C. as a symbol of Roman authority in Ephesus. The Ephesians lent support to Mithridates, king of Pontus, in his attempt to conquer the region in defiance of Rome. Having achieved his aim, he ordered a massacre of all Roman citizens in the region, in which, according to some sources, as many as 80,000 perished in a single night. This monument was erected as a memorial of this event.

FOUNTAIN OF POLLIO

This fountain, which dates from the 1st century A.D., was dedicated to Sextilius Pollio, who was responsible for the construction of the Marnas aqueduct. It has a concave facade. A sculpture group depicting one of the adventures of Ulysses discovered here was repaired and is now exhibited in the local museum.

TEMPLE OF DOMITIAN

A member of the Flavian dynasty, Domitian became Emperor in 81 A.D. At first an honest administrator he later became an tyrannical despot, proclaiming himself "Lord and God" (Dominus et Deus). Assassinated with the connivance of his wife Domitia, his memory was damned by decree of the senate (Damnatio memoriae) and all his statues destroyed.

Erected on a pseudodipteral plan with 8 x 13 columns, it was one of the largest temples in the city. A colossal statue was discovered here consisting of an arm with clenched fist made from a single piece of marble and a very well-preserved head. The temple and statue in Ephesus are of particularly great importance in view of the very few remains connected with Domitian.

44

The Council House and the Fountain of Pollio.

The Odeon.

PRYTANEION

Known as a place of worship dedicated to Artemis Boulaea, the Prytaneion was built during the reign of the Emperor Augustus, underwent repairs in the 3rd century and was destroyed at the end of the 4th. Here was to be found an urban sanctuary consisting of a square chamber paved with black and white marble containing an altar in a niche in front of which stood a figurine of the goddess Hestia, while the courtyard contained a statue of Athena. Here, too, burned the eternal flame symbolising the life of the city.

The large building consisted of a courtyard surrounded by porticos containing rooms and chambers, the colonnaded courtyard opening into a rectangular chamber with a roof supported by four Corinthian columns, three of which have survived. The building also had a secular function. The city administrators, foreign guests and local philanthropists would gather here to dine together. The famous statue of Artemis as goddess of plenty now exhibited in the museum was discovered here in absolutely perfect condition.

ODEUM

This building in the form of a small theatre was built in the 2nd century at around the same time and by the same people, namely Varius Antonius and his wife Flavia Papiona, as the baths beside it. It differs from the theatre in function, being used for meetings of the municipal council and concerts. It also differed from the theatre in being roofed by a wooden awning providing protection from sun and rain. It had seating for between 1500 and 2000. The first five tiers above the orchestra are original, with the stairs adorned with lion's paws in a very good state of preservation.

An extraordinarily beautiful head of Eros found in the orchestra area is now exhibited in the Selçuk Museum.

STATE AGORA

Investigations have shown that until the 4th century A.D. the site of the agora, where it was the custom to hold all types of political activity (elections, meetings, demonstrations, etc,), was occupied by a cemetery through which ran the sacred way. In the western section of this rectangular structure, three sides of which are surrounded by rows of columns, excavations have revealed the foundations of a 1st century temple dedicated to the cult of Isis. Between the state agora and the odeum lies a three-aisled roofed structure, 160 m in length, known as the Basilica. This is surrounded by three rows of columns with Corinthian and Ionic capitals adorned with bull's heads. This was used as the city bourse where money-lenders and bankers would meet to exchange money. It was completely destroyed at the end of the 6th century.

Beyond the state agora stands the Magnesian Gate, by which one leaves the ruins of Ephesus. Erected during the reign of Vespasian (69-79), in the form of a victory arch, this marks the beginning of the city walls surrounding the Panayir and Bülbül hills. On the left as you leave the gate you will see the eastern gymnasium, generally known as the WOMEN'S GYMNASIUM built by the Sophist Domianus and his wife Veda Faetrina in the 3rd century A.D. Excavations yielded a number of statues of young women providing very important evidence regarding the education of girls in ancient times. This is further corroborated by the inclusion of the name of a woman among the founders.

Cave of the Seven Sleepers.

CAVE OF THE SEVEN SLEEPERS

The inscriptions in this cave date from the 1st century, making them the earliest known Christian documents. According to Mecdelli, the Virgin Mary resided in Ephesus and was buried there. An inscription in ancient Greek to the effect that the famous believer known as St Feotini was buried in this cave was observed during excavations carried out by the Austrian team.

It was in this cave that seven young men are said to have gone to sleep during the reign of the Emperor Decius and wakened under the Christian Emperor Theodosius.

The cave is located in Mt Panayır at a point outside the defence walls erected by Lysimachus. The place seems to have been concealed. A different version of the legend appears in the Qur'an.

HOUSE OF THE VIRGIN MARY

Anatolia has been the home of a great variety of civilisations and faiths, and the house of the Virgin Mary is one of the most important of the places that bear witness to the evolution of human belief. It is located about 4 km from the Magnesian Gate in the ancient city of Ephesus in a spot fairly difficult of access at a height of 358 m on the summit of a hill.

It enjoys an exceptionally fine climate with a lovely view over an extraordinarily beautiful countryside. The only sound is the song of the birds, and its height removes it from the scorching heat of the Ephesus plain. It affords a magnificent bird's eye view of the surrounding region, extending to a horizon where the earth embraces the blue of the sky.

House of the Virgin Mary.

After parking your vehicle and making your way past the pool on the left used for collecting water, you will see a panel on the right with information for visitors in several languages. Just after this, on the left, a little before the actual house, the Virgin Mary patiently and lovingly awaits you with out-stretched arms. This bronze statue was discovered in excavations carried out at the beginning of the 19th century and the broken arm repaired. A few paces further on you will come to the house of the Virgin Mary under a cluster of plane trees. Whether this is actually the spot where the Virgin Mary spent her last days and from which she finally ascended to heaven is a question still hotly debated by scholars, but the whole story is based on a strong tradition to be found among the old citizens of Ephesus and the local inhabitants. Dom Ruinart (1657-1707), Baronius (1528-1607), Tillemont

(1637-1698) and Pope Benoit XIV (1675-1758) all agree that St John the Apostle took Mary to Asia Minor between the years 37 and 45.

It was long the custom for local Christians to make their way to "Panaghia Kapoulu", the chapel hidden in the mountains, to celebrate the Dormition of the Virgin. They firmly believed in the tradition handed down to them from previous generations that this is where the Virgin spent her last days.

In the 19th century, a bed-ridden German invalid by the name of Catherine Emmerich (1774-1824) wrote a book entitled *La Vie de la Sainte Vierge* under what she claimed was divine inspiration. Although she had never visited the region she described it with astounding accuracy, placing the chapel on top of the hill, and it was thanks to this book and the information it contained that the Lazarist priests of the Church of St Polycarp

House of the Virgin Mary.Interior.

The Artemission.

in Izmir succeeded in identifying the spot.

There are several other facts that may be taken as evidence that the Virgin Mary once lived here.

* The existence of the tomb of St. John, who is known to have died in Ephesus and been buried in the place where we have remains of the Basilica dedicated to him. The Basilica was constructed under the Byzantine Emperor Justinian in the 6th century AD. The Basilica is located very near the Isa Bey Mosque in Selçuk.

* The Third Ecumenical council was held in Ephesus. In the year 431 A.D. and in the year 449 the so-called Robber Council took place in Ephesus.

* The Double Church of the Virgin in Ephesus is the oldest church dedicated to the Virgin Mary.

* The epistles written by St Paul to the Ephesians.

* The location of the story of the Seven Sleepers in Ephesus.

In 1892 Mgr.Tomoniu, the Archbishop of Izmir, pronounced the House of the Virgin Mary a place of pilgrimage.

Finally, in view of the unanimous historical evidence, the house was also accepted as a place of pilgrimage by the Vatican. Archaeologists who have examined the building corroborate the above evidence, pointing to striking resemblances to the chapel in 6th century use, while some of the walls can be dated to the 1st century. Moreover, the archaeologists found 1.2 m3 of petrified ashes in the hearth. There is also the pool, which would appear to have been regarded by visitors as sacred.

Whatever the final conclusion, this simple house, restored and converted into a chapel, has, since 1951, attracted pilgrims of every religion and every race.

ARTEMISION
THE MOTHER GODDESS,
ARTEMIS OF THE EPHESIANS

Artemis is the name given to a divinity worshipped for centuries in the Mediterranean world. Kubala, recognised as Mother Goddess throughout the whole of Mesopotamia,was referred to in the Phrygian language as Kybele. The cult of the goddess had spread from Anatolia to Mesopotamia, Syria, Lebanon and Palestine, thence to Egypt and from the Aegean Islands to Crete. It can also be traced in Greece and Italy as well as in the northern countries. This goddess, who symbolised the soil and its fruitfulness and the fertility of nature, was worshipped under various names at various times and in various places. Although there is no definite information regarding the development of this cult in Ephesus, Artemis is clearly regarded in the Homeric eulogy as an Ionian goddess.

One of the constant attributes of the goddess is the number three. Artemis is regarded as virgin, wife and mother. "The whole of nature was subject to this primitive goddess. It is by her orders that the earth brings forth fruit and flowers. She rules the elements, the air, the earth and the sea. She governs the life of the animals, she tames the wild beasts and prevents their extinction.... She assists in birth. Homer calls her "the goddess of wild animals". Artemis became the tutelary goddess of Marsilia, Carthage and the cities of the Near East. As the ruler of civilisation she wore a head-dress crowned with city towers. Each year, she was celebrated almost everywhere in great festivals as the fertility goddess and granted innumerable prayers. She was described as the "bee goddess" and on one side of the

The Artemission.

Ephesus coins was to be found the queen bee as the symbol of Artemis. The hymn written by Callimachos to Artemis ends with a sentence describing the Amazon dance. "Let no one refrain from the annual dance of Artemis". The annual festival of Artemis lasted for a month, during which time people came pouring into Ephesus from the four corners of the known world to take part in the entertainments, dances and commercial activities."

The first temple dedicated to Artemis was completed in 625 B.C and destroyed during the Cimmerian invasions.

According to Pliny, this imposing building was destroyed and rebuilt nine times. This archaic building possessed marble columns, some of which were donated by Croesus, King of Lydia. An older building was unearthed with the same plan and dimensions, remains from which are now preserved in the British Museum. Three other floors belonging to the old building were unearthed by David George Hogarth, who was in charge of the excavations carried out here in 1904-1906 on behalf of the same museum. The coins discovered in the lowest floor date from the 6th century B.C. The later Artemision was built in 564-540 B.C. The most distinguished artists and architects of the day, Scopas, Praxiteles, Polycleitos, Phidias, Cresilas, Cydon and Apellas,, combined to produce a magnificent building four times the size of the Parthenon in Athens. Appeles was responsible for the picture "Aphrodite Anadiomene" within the temple. According to Pliny's *Naturalis Historia,* this was an Ionic temple measuring 200 x 425 m with 127 columns reaching a height of 20 m.

Regarded as one of the Seven Wonders of the World, the building is said to have been destroyed by a madman by the name of Herostratos who burned down the temple in order to immortalise his name. Alexander the Great, on his way to the Persian campaign,

offered to defray the expenses of the restoration of the building provided he might be permitted to make the dedicatory inscription in his own name, but the Ephesians declined the offer on the grounds that it was not fitting for a temple to be dedicated to two gods, thus refusing the offer without hurting his pride. The new temple, built in the years 334-260 B.C., was the largest Greek temple then in existence.

It was erected on the foundations of the older temple and was thus exactly the same size, but owing to the marshy nature of the land it was raised on a *crepidoma* of sixteen steps. It lay on an east-west axis on a peninsula surrounded on three sides by the sea with sacred harbours, allowing ships to be moored directly to the steps of the temple. The architects of the first building built by Croesus were Chersiphron and Metesenes, while Critocrates and Oritocrates are said to have been the architects responsible for the 4th century B.C. building. The temple was detroyed by the invading Goths in 262 A.D. and never rebuilt. The Temple of Artemis was a prototype of the Ionic style. The Artemision was first and foremost a religious institution. A large number of priests and priestesses lived in the temple. Coins were minted there, credit given and a type of banking carried out.

Festivities were held in May each year to celebrate the birthday of the goddess. Until the spread of Christianity and monotheism, Ephesus was a place of pilgrimage. Moreover, all sorts of criminals and wrong-doers found sanctuary in the temple, whose sanctity was respected by all the rulers of Western Anatolia. When St Paul arrived in Ephesus preaching a belief in one god, he was confronted by the Ephesians chanting their slogan "Great is Artemis of the Ephesians", but when, in the Christian era, the worship of their goddess was finally prohibited, they transferred some of the attributes of Artemis to the Virgin Mary.

Ephesian Artemis (Ephesus Museum).

The village of Şirince (Ayasoluk).

EXCAVATIONS

The first temple was unearthed in excavations carried out on behalf of the British Museum in 1869-74 by J.T.Wood, who was employed at that time on the construction of the railroad. A corner of the temple was discovered in 1869. The finds were transported first to Izmir then via Venice to London. At the present day the most important of the finds from the temple are preserved in the British Museum. According to old sources some of the architectural elements from the temple were employed in the construction of the basilica of Ayasofya.

AYASOLUK TEPESI
HAGHIOS THEOLOGOS

This is the site of the ancient city acropolis. In the course of time it assumed the form of an alternative settlement and, after the silting up of the harbours had reduced the importance of Ephesus as a port, the Byzantines built a castle on Ayasoluk Tepesi. After its capture by the Seljuks in the 11th century the hill changed hands several times between the Byzantines and the Anatolian Seljuks, finally emerging in 1438 as a commercial centre subject to the Aydınoğulları. It was finally incorporated into Ottoman territory in 1402. It came under Greek occupation in the years 1919 to 1922. Since 1957 it has formed part of the province of Izmir.

During the 19th century the centre of

Views of the Church of St. John.

administration was transferred for a time from Ayasuluk to the large Greek village ŞİRİNCE.

ISA BEY MOSQUE

This is a Seljuk-Turkish building erected in 1375 by Isa Bey, the founder of the Aydınoğulları Emirate. It is an interesting example of asymmetrical architecture. The courtyard of the mosque was formerly surrounded by a gallery surmounted by domes, now no longer in existence. All the windows were in the same style. The marble carving is of the highest quality. The courtyard was later used as a cemetery.

THE CHURCH OF ST JOHN THE EVANGELIST

The disciple most beloved of Christ and the only disciple to be present at the

Views of the Church of St. John.

crucifixion, St John was entrusted by Christ with the care of His mother, the Virgin Mary. He later played a very important role in the dissemination of Christianity and wrote the Apocalypse during the reign of the Emperor Domitian (81-96 A.D.) to raise the morale of a people terrorized by persecution and oppression. The Apocalypse was included in the New Testament as the last book in the collection. It is generally agreed that he resided in Ephesus following his return from exile on the island of Patmos around 100 A.D. The first church to bear his name was built over his grave some years after his death but the great basilica is ascribed to the reign of the Emperor Justinian in the 6th century. According to investigations carried out on the burial chamber in 1926-28, the church was constructed over an older church of the 4th century. It was finally abandoned after the conquest of the area by the Seljuks in the 13th century, and was burned and destroyed during the Mongol raids of 1402.

The building measures 40 x 110 m and is aligned on an east-west axis with the entrance on the western side. On the northern side on the left of the basilica there is a small chapel with frescos dated to the 11th century. Immediately to the left of this room, which was used by the priests as a vestry, there is a small treasury in which valuable holy relics were kept. The baptistery was found in a good state of preservation and has since been restored. It is now known that this section existed before the church itself. Investigations have revealed column capitals belonging to the Emperor Justinian and his wife Theodora.

Selçuk, Isa Bey Mosque.

Selçuk Castle.

Marble busts in the Ephesus Museum. The Emperor Aurelius 3rd century A.D., The Emperor Trajan 3rd century A

The Resting Warrior 1st century A.D.

...ad of a man 2nd century A.D., The God Zeus 1st century A.D., Socrates Roman Period.

SELÇUK CASTLE

The castle is situated on a hill to the north of the church. It is a Byzantine structure, repaired during the Aydınoğulları Emirate, which displays building techniques of various periods. The perimeter measures nearly 1.5 km. There are fifteen bastions and a mosque dating from the 14th century.

ARCHAEOLOGICAL MUSEUM

Although relatively small, this is one of the richest and most important museums in Turkey. It consists of six exhibition rooms and a courtyard.

SALON I: Finds from the Terrace Houses. The exhibits in this room include a of Dolphin and Cupid, a head of Eros, a figurine of Priapus, a head of Socrates, a wall painting and the statue of a priest.

SALON II: Finds from the fountain.

The main exhibits in this room are the statues from the facades of the fountain of Polio and the fountain of Trajan, statues of the river-god Triton and a number of busts.

SALON III: Antique coins.

Gold ornaments and coins and medallions bearing a representation of the bee, one of the most important symbols of the city of Ephesus.

INNER COURTYARD (ATRIUM): Finds from the Belevi Funeral Monument, fragments from the Artemision, a sundial and very interesting bull-head columns.

SALON IV: Burial chamber finds, 6th century sarcophagus, vessels for ashes and vessels used in burial ceremonies.

SALON V: Finds from the Temple of

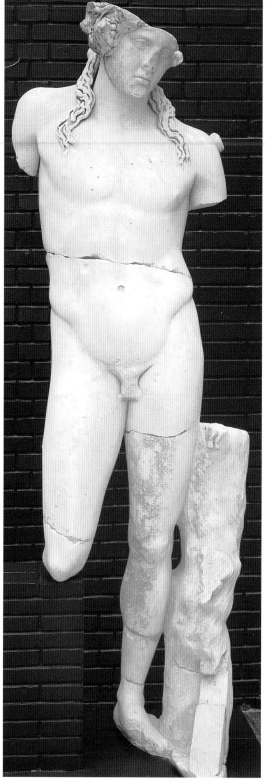

Ephesian Artemis.

Statue of Dionysus.

Marble Sarcophagus (detail).

Emperor Domitian.

Artemis. Two unique statues of the goddess
and other finds from the temple.

SALON VI: The room of the Emperors.
Finds from the temples of Hadrian and
Domitian.

EPHESUS

CONTENTS

Published and Distributed by
REHBER Basım Yayın Dağıtım Reklamcılık ve Tic. A.Ş.
Dolapdere Cad. No:106, Şişli İstanbul - TURKEY
Tel: (90-212) 230 22 65   Fax: (90-212) 231 33 50

Photos : Erdal Yazıcı, Güngör Özsoy, Halûk Özözlü, Tahsin Aydoğmuş
Graphic and Layout : Ulaş Şensilay
Typsetting : AS & 64 Ltd. Şti.
Printed Turkey by Lebib Yalkın Matbaası.

ISBN 975-6671-44-0